Winner of the L. E. Phillabaum Poetry Award for 2008

Slantwise

POEMS
Betty Adcock

LOUISIANA STATE UNIVERSITY PRESS BATON ROUGE

NATIONAL ENDOWMENT FOR THE ARTS   This publication is supported in part by an award from the
National Endowment for the Arts.

Published by Louisiana State University Press
Copyright © 2008 by Betty Adcock
All rights reserved
Manufactured in the United States of America
First printing

DESIGNER: Barbara Neely Bourgoyne
TYPEFACES: Myriad Pro, display; Minion Pro, text
PRINTER AND BINDER: Thomson-Shore, Inc.

Thanks to the editors of the following publications, in which some of these poems first ap-
peared, sometimes under different titles or in slightly different versions: *Atlanta Review,* "*Ars
Poetica* on an Island in the Cyclades" (Fall/Winter 2002); *Chautauqua Literary Journal,* "It's
déjà vu all over again" (2004); *Margie,* "Day Lilies" (Fall 2005); *neo,* "Gladys in Springtime,"
"Tree Man" (both Spring 2007); *North Carolina Literary Review,* "House Cats" (1998); *Pleiades,*
"Chimneys: A History of Deep East Texas" (2006); *Ploughshares,* "Roustabout" (Spring 2008);
Shenandoah, "Little Text" (Summer 2002); *Smartish Pace,* "Rare" (No. 12); *Southern Review,*
"Kind of Blue," "No Elegy in November" (both Autumn 2002); *Tar River Poetry,* "Diagnosis"
(Fall 2003), "To Mollie Siju Ruinsky, Granddaughter in the Air" (Spring 2006); *Virginia
Quarterly Review,* "Why White Southern Poets Write the Way We Do" (Winter 2004).

"Antinomy" first appeared in the *Raleigh News and Observer.* "Day Lilies" was originally
commissioned by ELM Press and appeared in the limited-edition art book *Ars Botanica*
(2005). "Little Text" appeared in the *Pushcart Prize Anthology XXVIII.*

Thanks to Meredith College, to North Carolina State University, and to Claudia Emerson,
Tim McBride, and Julie Suk.

My deepest thanks to the John Simon Guggenheim Foundation for the fellowship that
made this book possible and supported the research for my next project.

Library of Congress Cataloging-in-Publication Data
Adcock, Betty.
  Slantwise : poems / Betty Adcock.
    p. cm.
  Includes bibliographical references.
  ISBN 978-0-8071-3309-5 (cloth : alk. paper) — ISBN 978-0-8071-3310-1 (pbk. : alk. paper)
  I. Title.
  PS3551.D396S63 2008
  813'.54—dc22

                                        2007034191

The paper in this book meets the guidelines for permanence and durability of the Committee
on Production Guidelines for Book Longevity of the Council on Library Resources. ∞

This book is for Don,
Sylvia and Steve,
Tai and Mollie

Contents

Slantwise

Little Text

East Texas

1

One needle from a longleaf pine
left over from logging, one
needle falling through green
shade, through warp and shimmer of
September sometimes
                              end over end will
turn as if marking the passing
air with form, circumference
as of time's real motion or
the approximation of, say,
a face.

Which way the needle rests,
'possum or 'coon or wildcat
may pick up, taking on
this compass with its freight
of indication and downturning
invisible incident. It will be

passenger only until shed
onto briar or buttonbush, being only
a downed, straitened angel,
pin and linear argument,
line of prophecy flattened letterless
whose browning measure
                              beneath notice
points both ways at once—
though its done, erratic circle
(like the aftermath of water around

1

a pebble) may widen
likewise to horizon
where it could shine the way
scripture shines, or spider's orb
or the water-drop
                    tinctured with sky.
It could be shining.

2

I may have come for just this,
so long gone I can't remember bare
footlogs across the gar-infested creeks
or the heron thrust up white for magic,
for instructions
                    hidden
in the hollow wingbone.

And the scissortail has cleft this light
with journeys all my distant life.

Under a stranded palmetto,
the armadillo's metal is unzipped,
the flesh burst toward that further
wandering in earth where move
the multitudes,
                    and into air
where memory breathes its midge-cloud.

Thus unstitched, time will wander,
and the pine needle (beneath, now,
a boot) has left on air a print
of the suddenly upstanding huge
guessed-at virgin tree,
and a feather, drifting, says

bird in a small stir
against the cheek,
                    barn swallow
hawk-snatched from the sky, redtail
gone, gone by.

    3

It all happened, it happened
all in glassclear air.

And now? This present chainsaw-battered
earth, town-rent, tracked and fired
with pitiful need,
                    this water
displaced and broken into use.

The air smeared with smoke, with
gunpowder and history, the obsolete
intentions of factories, with a grease
redolent of human hope: air here
might hold faintly, as on a fading
photographic plate,
                    a naked
walking child, bark-colored women
with baskets woven of long grass and pine
needles, roots in the baskets—
                              and not far
a battle wearing
                    red clay
and berrystain and bearfat. There
a cougar rises to threaten the two-footed
fighters, our feet
                    in those tracks.

4

What am I but the visible door
onto that corridor incarnate with the ache
of cypress and ty-vine, raccoon and fox,
bat and buzzard, hanged man, red child,
world flesh sutured with our small past,
inscription after inscription missed
or grasped dreamlike in the unsteady
sensing the body is. And the body is
already arcing backward, describing,
darkening into path.

DANCERS

Dancers

Because we were the last ones deserted
by the God of visions and serpents—

because a summer field can levitate
on the ratcheting din of cicadas—

because the magnolia, offering its melted candles,
burns invisible prayers into sunlight—

because every one of us has at least one
relative who plowed poor with a mule—

because the dead still enter our sleep as columns
of figures on the debit side of the ledger,

and darker voices carry what we cannot speak:
black ghosts, smoke in the twilit live oaks—

because we found broken words everywhere
rolling like loose beads under the chiffonier,

and we weren't suspicious when our breath
restrung them in patterns heavy as Scripture—

because a mist can sit in a pasture
like a cloud in a basket—

because we never stopped believing the hoop snake
actually does assert the compass of time
pursuing the vanished, the exiled dreamers,

even as we rise to occasion almost
reprieved,
            the way weed-strangled fields
rise in colors of October fire, in the one
celebration we're given:
to dance, to sing anyhow, to grieve.

BARRIER ISLANDS

Skirts of the continent, ruffled in heavy pavane
of sand and tide or frenzied in capriccios
of gales, can sometimes tear like lace in the turns
as of dancers wearing the wind, wearing the moon.

Salt-drenched beloved of the hurricane,
their drift is longer than the sea's *step in,
step out;* partners the storm but answers
no augur.
        Edgy, we say,
of something new. *Cutting edge,* we say.

This power's like the slow velocities
of art, shape-shifting stillness, all time
in motion, all motion
                trying to be form.

TREE MAN

He hangs from a pinnacle—
                              pin oak—
at seventy feet, its hundred years hold
him by strap and barbed boots when the huge
branches let go under sawteeth. They break
in a little drumbeat of twigs and falling
ivy vine, then the singular *thud* of earth-grown
weight returning.

And there he leans to wave, to curtsey,
to cut a figure like a skater on the air.
He gestures, hangs by one hand, jumps up
to tap across a branch big as a small bridge.
Gandy dancer in reverse, he removes
the tracks laid down by all those years
in the deep whorls of the heart,
behind him only the blue sky

emptying now. He's a high sparkle
of red in his jumpsuit, his long
hair flying, four limbs jiving
up there to stay alive. He tips
his hardhat, then turns intent
to the destruction he's best at,
the joy of that.

1932

for my mother, Sylvia (1902–1944)
and my father, Ralph (1904–1974)

Come from elsewhere to teach in our town,
she was thirty, tall, with a willowy figure,
waves of black hair, black eyes. My father
fell in love: heart   soul   blood   bone.

He courted the schoolteacher long and long.
He brought roses and letters, says the storyteller.
He brought a hand-cranked gramophone.
And on one exquisitely unfettered

night they took that machine and its forlorn
love songs down to the Carize Creek bridge,
set it on the bridge rail and turned and turned
until music and the May moon leapt the ridge

of pines, and the stars came out, and the mild air
filled up with music, a world entire.
Then (spied on by children who reported back)
he held her close, their season intact.

See them?
            The deer have run from a foreign thing.
There's no automobile out this late.
The horned owl complains and does not stay
where they and their lantern-light are dancing.

He kisses her. Perhaps they lie down
together on the spring-warmed ground?
No. They dance (only dance) the little span
of time that stretches from *then* to *then.*

She died the year I was six, taking with her
my remembering: face, words, hands, the shining hair.
For years, his grief kept all questions away.
What happened before I was born? Who were they?

I hold this memory not mine. There's nothing
I know except that he lost her, and I lost them both;
yet now they dance with the marvelous moon
that dwarfs their lantern. I hear them hum

along with a scratchy saccharine tune
from that poverty-ridden American year,
and she turns and turns in the arms of my father
toward the calling light of their broken future.

> One of the family that boarded my mother
> has told me this story: all that I have
> of their early knowing one another.
> I know the place, the bridge, the rough
> enclosing forest. It shines.
>   It is enough.

I was twenty-two, pretty maybe. It was a small town
county fair: hot dogs, freak show, cotton candy,
and heavy wheels laden with light,
all tuned to the gaudy air.

The Octopus—remember that one? Eight
arms like extended girders, the thing was a metal
Shiva juggling worlds: a cup spun at the end
of each madly oscillating arm, every cup
overfull of squealing kids or lovers drunk
on the whip-sharp unexpected torque
toward the expected rapture.

He was maybe twenty, bare-chested, tanned
and gleaming in the southern September night,
a kind of summer in the lights that played
across him as he pulled levers set to arm
the bright contraption with speed and plunge,
with whirl and rise. His hair was almost red
in the lights' translation. Not many
riders yet, when suddenly he leapt
onto one of the metal arms in its low sweep
and rose with it. And laughed.

I thought it might be for me, this showing
off. He jumped onto the next arm as it rose,
went up with it, then landed easy on the ground.
He vaulted the lowered ones as they went by,
stepped up again, and down again, then ducked
under so a steel arm grazed his cap. How long
ago it was.

How long did I stand and watch
that wild control before I turned
to find my husband and my child?

He's likely dead now. Or deep asleep
in some wine-dark room, some ragged dream.
I think no golden years follow that life,
though I still see him shining new
against black sky and turning stars—
chancing it, taking on the monster,
winning, dancing it.

The window beside my desk has taken on
a bright distorting surface: aquarium glass
alive with what's behind it, and transformed.
Oaks and maples in the yard are tossed
in the wavering fingers of October sun
flinging their leaves to brilliance in the turn
now one way, now another—darting pattern
schooled in a light gone aqueous, gone

into the old dream-dance of figuration
the world with us performs. This sleight of wind
has caught the season brightness gathers.
Leaves and fishes fill the eye with mind
and conjugate with water as light and air,
as if earth itself still hungered for the word.

No Elegy in November

for A.W.H.

They will not turn, the dead,
from their ashen lace or outward-facing
stone. Having fled along the route
all planetary matter takes, they race—
like light from its creation—

invincibly away. No backward look
brings them again to being,
no salt embrace
freezes their going.
                    They take
with them form and gesture,
all that we're graced to know
of permanence and change.

You left us in a turbulence, your time
a dazzlement of ruffled silk and feathers,
confusions of anger and refusal, a music
always discordant and beautiful together.
And, as you meant it to,
the drama you had set us in played on.

Unkindling utterly, you will not turn
nor send your wildfire spirit back to speak.
You'll not forgive, nor longer wish, nor see
how you have left the rest of us to burn.

Told by the Madwoman Who Stopped Making Quilts

Once, the strip of dusk I saw through
a window matched exactly the small stripe
in a piece of silk I'd kept. *Naked peach,*
I called it. A little deeper and it would have been
that odd shade city sunsets show so prettily—
they say pollution makes it, but it shines
a sweet sheen before dark. Once I pieced a whole quilt
of such dangerous affects; like Joseph's coat,
an inspired treachery. I named that one *Maybe.*
Always I made crazy quilts, the kind that honor
wild thought or happenstance or war.

I learned the old, good names of dyes and pigments:
cerulean, viridian sharp as filed iron, *vermilion*
like a sunstorm. Every one of them alive, even brown
that seeing alone will turn just plain or sad;
but saying creates it *cordovan* or *sepia, dun*
or *burnt sienna,* even *rufous* or *alizarin.*
None of what you'd guess a pair of muddy shoes
to be, or the drab coat you saw on some poor woman
in the street, or the hands of an old man the color
of a cap of baby's lace gone dark in time.

That woman's coat, now . . .
I have been known to snip a bit from
people's clothes right where they sit
on a park bench or in a movie house,
on a bar stool or a shoe-store chair.
Dim church pews are best if you are careful.
It's where people wear their finery and are still.
The scissors must be very small. You can't get
ambitious.

I got good at moveless work,
gathering little jots of cloth to improvise
a pattern with. I might call one quilt *Stained
Mass,* another *You Guess Where* or *They Died.*
You could always take the titles how you liked.

Cobalt sounds like lightning, don't you think?
Satin holds that flicker. I saw close lightning
once, and it wasn't yellow-red but a singeing blue.
And I love the *acid yellows* of October,
then early leaves the red of *hematite*
that goes to orange. Means blood. I like
blind depths of *cochineal* the popes
in paintings wear—what that means
who knows?
                    Perhaps the same.

I gathered figured fabrics and splashes
of single color, vivid sparks
the world threw off. I filled my days
with baskets of the past, small thievings,
taking part in life by taking part
of it to make it art.
                    The very word
dye implies a fastness, a permanence.
But hear how it echoes the one command
we're sure God gave us? Such things matter.

You know it's said that colors are the children
of the light. Then, like all children,
they must be frightened of the dark.
And isn't fire (that holds the whole
wide spectrum in the sun) our light most perfect?
That mordant fixes the awful *all* of things
fast, fast to this world, each for its moment.

Something like that's how I came to do it,
without being able to recount exactly why.
I piled all my quilts in the backyard,
piled them head-high, my life's pieces
and the lives of others, parsed,
broken palette, constellation of the random.
But line to line appropriately made—
the way a voice is moving and the same.

I circled
the shining hill with lightwood, turning
to build a kindling fence. And then,
I lit the circle.

(Black, they say, is the color that exists
only in the imagination.)

The center brightened first,
past *ocher*'s paleolithic
shadow, to *saffron* and *copper blue; azurum*
and sudden *dragon's blood, cerise,* even
Van Gogh's poisonous *Naples yellow.*
The color wheel kept turning in its fire
until it streamed into a dance of mourning veils—
the sound of that
was a flock of winging birds caught fast
in the blinding net of likeness and these words.

Antinomy

Snowflakes, which muffle sound in air, actually squeal in water . . .
It's deafening to creatures such as porpoises that can hear the very
high frequencies. "It would be like a screech . . . like the difference
between conversation and a rock band concert," said Lawrence
Crum of the Applied Physics Laboratory.
    —Associated Press, January 28, 2000

The moon webbed in snowfall goes rising
over the stockstill world, all
night shedding silver after silver
dress among shadows, on the buried
grass and the willow's
arrested fountain.

This mountainous quiet, towering
over the fields, could shroud and muffle
the murderer's footfall. The owl's eye
is its window, all silence, silence
as of one who'd slip in to undo
a sleeper with blade edge or pillow.

The white tiptoe of winter,
when it falls onto water,
goes roaring, a substanceless
noise harsh as an avalanche.
Spokes of the snowflakes are knives
of iced air. They flower just under
the waterskin:
                    explosions
of nothingness into high bedlam,
a tangle of languages plumbing
the salt dark layered on dark.

Then the shark
grinds his teeth;
whales fear and collide;
and the porpoise
warps in his course.

Panic leaves hiding
as wave becomes Babel,
abysmal down-reaching
screeching in frequencies
the drowned in their fathoms
might hear (if
they hear there)
as the return of their wars.

So laden with snow, the brightening
dark carries
          a sweet-feathered whisper,
          an unblunted keening:
the lace of old chaos.

Day Lilies

Called *ditchflowers,* they call all summer
day   day   day   day   their drumbeat
drawn out of dawn that lifts from green sleep
the tiger's orange, soft melon and peach,
cadmium yellow, carmine, coral pink,
ivory pale as a corpse's cheek—a range
so wide and subtle they might fabricate a dye wheel.

To rise again their one completion, mayflies
in stasis, they likewise last
                          one turn around
the sundial, and are so fast replaced no one imagines
when yesterday slipped, pleated with shadow,
into a fading curl.
                          The buds are long thin furlings
of crumpled silk, with only a glance of color
but ready to break into daybreak and rocket rubescent
into noon, trumpeting remarkable ancestry.

For their progenitors are at least as old as Egypt's
tomb walls holding paintings of white flared
tumblers filled with light: the lilies of the field
we're asked to consider. Consider them:
first flowers to come in from the wild;
the first to soothe, to celebrate, perhaps the first
thought to comfort the dead whose eternal dark
would be only the sleep of winter for these
recurring suns.

The originals were fists full of tomorrows,
knots of plumbless metaphor: Hera's milk
and the Silk Road to come, the imperial Regal,

and the medieval paintbrush clotted
with piety, tracing the Virgin's purity
against her skyblue cloak.
                    Only old dreams, the thousands
of new names that play now in the garden's mouth,
the countless, cloudless colors climbing the world
for beauty and brevity, knowing always
    one day   one day   one day   this
                                one day.

ASIDES

Diagnosis

Perhaps we die of an overload of stories.
Too many sagas, memories, jokes, pantomimes;
too much melodrama, history lived or teased
out of the inexhaustible.
There's the truth about our parents. And
the way the West was really won; why the chicken
crossed the road. And what my neighbor said
when she went mad.
                                    Then there's the epic
of matter imagining itself: the latest dream
mammalian. Underneath, the bone-deep nightmare
of techtonic travel. And there's that
tallest tale of an expanding
universe, or a contracting one. Or
the invisible black weight that is
the finish of a star.
                                    Earlier,
youth kept us safe:
no room in us for all that, for so many
verbs, so many distraught and pushy adjectives,
armies of vowels and consonants; no room
for so many perilous serials.

I'm sitting now in the low backyard
where moss outdoes the grass.
It's July again too quickly. Fireflies
have begun their obstinate questioning.
Remember how we used to catch them, the jar
we'd put them in, the lively lights
so clearly dying and coming back?

Maybe the stories that live in us
collect the way newspapers and books fill up
the house of the lunatic, chaos through
which some path must be incised—the body
so full of profoundly *more* than blood
and bones, cholesterol and carcinogens,
fat and shit and the makings of desire.

My half-Indian great-grandmother sits
in my knees, an ache like too much prayer.
The madwoman gone from next door
is a mutter in my wrists. The spinster who made
bread for us children—she spread every slice
with the word of a wrathful God—lives now
in dreams I still recount. I'm trying yet
to find that dark jam sweet.
There was a man in our town whose baby boy
was taken up into the mouth of a tornado
and set down unharmed in the middle of a road—
what to do with that one, its ungainly
angles resolving with such grace,
its cry of surprise?
I had a relative who killed a man
and ran off to Chicago with his father's
money, never again heard from.
                                    None of them
heroes, not one of them more than
particular, outlined briefly against cosmic
night and geologic time.

Perhaps the stories are what we come
at last to be ourselves, the sum of them
what we come finally to understand,
along with atoms and the many extinctions:
dinosaurs and wolves, ivorybills and whales.

Is it then that we can begin to love
the world before us, all our ghosts
with their changing outlines
showing like petticoats?

                              All that we never
asked to know can enter the body, can enter
and fill and stay. My spine weakens
under the weight of another great-grandmother
who saw her daughter raped in a Georgia cornfield
by Union soldiers. The wagon she drove alone
with her five children to Texas
shakes my marrow loose.

Understand, if I try to give them away
they will hide and pretend the way icebergs
are deep under sunlit water. I have to
carry them. They go before me
like breath you can see when it's cold.
I hold them in me like coals in a basket,
like a summer's quick-winging lights
in a casket of glass.

Spells

1

To take back what time has taken from you,
go into woods at autumn. Creekwater there
will be black and the diamondcutter
sun will break it still
where a quilt of leaves dapples the water
red and yellow. Unstitched and afloat,
that changeable pattern becomes the bed
of your childhood, the dream you so deeply
believed could warm all darkness. Notice
every bead of the light strung
on the flight of the blue heron.

Say it.

2

I broke a gift of November leaves to bring,
these imperfect ones, their colors
blotched toward winter.
There's a depth in them that's near
the distinctions of old wood without the lasting.
Wind they answered green has got inside them.
There's a reason for my choosing
this gift you'll have to lose.

Look close.

Fallen

The space shuttle *Columbia* broke up over several East Texas counties, including sparsely populated San Augustine County, on the morning of February 1, 2003.

Silver the winter morning, silver
the early sun downpouring
onto columns of pine and oak, miles
of birdsong-piercing silence silver
in the hour just before the rain;
and our shining myth oncoming, loosening
piecemeal overhead a ghastly charivari
in the high branches, mayhem broken
from the seared-off caul of cold space.

Imagine the torn, deer-haunted woods
where a severed foot still in its boot
was driven into mud. Imagine rags of flesh,
the heart found near a logging road,
the arm in underbrush, insignia beside
an upended helmet filling with icy rain.

Buzzards led the searchers—
                           don't recoil—do
not imagine this a story to be tamed by naming
heroes who died for country and some further bourne
worth dying for.
                 Don't imagine this as anything
beyond the old arc snapped, covenant entirely
broken, our ships no more than silver needles
trying the boundless haystacks of the stars.

Those shadow-stories people lived within
(when we were only hurt and poorly wise)
have hardened into nightmare: heaven
as fleshly destination, hell a fire
we make on earth where myth and science
change partners in the dance.

Only thin February light could plumb the deep
East Texas forests, men combing miles of underbrush
for the whole bloody puzzle, every shard
of failed metal and all the flesh it failed.
Among enormous trees, on a red clay road,
Chinquapin Baptist Church—chosen
beyond all prophecy and imagining—became
receiving station for the shattered dead.

Of course exhausted searchers didn't exhaust
that arboreous dark, its snarled thickets,
its hawk-sharpened air.
                              Light-footed foxes live there,
wildcats, the invisible cougar, wild boar
winter-thin and hungry, and shuffling armadillos
better armored than the astronauts sent out
as latter knights to press
our argument with airlessness
and make a grail of the mirage our image is,
among the novas and the planetary shrugs.

Disarticulate as temples seized by jungle,
this journey too will disappear. For a while
a mangled piece of the spaceship's hull
swung high in a shagbark hickory,
            bell calling what faithful
                        to the altar of the owl?

Backyard: Evening Variations

Late June spins a thickening twilight, birdsong
threading needlepoint through the weave of heat
and lengthened shadow. The thrush's madrigal,
rilling silver along the rising dark,
stitches summer's flowers on
the long train-whistle's dopplered ribbon.

The long train-whistle's doppler ribbons
tiger lily's going day, blood-rust zinnia,
sunflower fringes troubled with finches.
A cardinal chips as if at granite-colored
cloud. To what island do they go
when the world is out of light?

When light is gone, where do the birds go?
In full night, all green leaves disappear—
only the birch trunks vivid, as if moonrise
brought an errant winter to snatch them bare.
Watch how the sun goes raveling down
waves of suddenly brilliant clouds, drowning

all that is not cloud and color. That's when
the vanishing speak their exit: towhee's
torqued query, bluejay's final quip,
the thrush's braiding-downward fountain
ceasing.
          Now the bat's high notice warps
and wimples. Now fireflies prophesy.

The one loom fabricates, again, the stars.

Seeing Josephine

Either we lived in paradise or it was hell
covered over, sodded with flowers—

now after more than half a century, you've called
on my rare visit home. You cry and embrace
a woman who can't recall your childhood face.
We're family, you tell me. I don't say
the music of your name is all I kept:
Jo-se-phine, Jo-se-phine, I'd sing out
down the stairs, a syllable a step.

I do remember how we ranged the pecan grove,
holding in our hands the firefly flares
of summer. Puppies tumbled in the yard,
a calf in the pasture. Pomegranates weighted
our autumn afternoons, ripe muted suns

that never lit the world behind the world,
behind the henyard where the cabin leaned
(where you were born) whose rough doorstep
I never crossed. Empty now with more
than empty air, I imagine its boards grained
with pleading, a shouted No! and the groan
of a white man who'd come late and left at dawn.
I imagine the sounds a birth makes when it kills
the mother.
                    But all I have is guesswork.

One summer the dogs went rabid, I remember that,
but what do I know of history? It was papered over
like that cabin's drafty boards. Lets in the rain.
Lets in the layered wind. Lets in

a story that falls on me in small droplets,
that makes a little rivulet like a vine, there
and not there, ghostly serpentine glimpse
as through a curtain.

Black Josephine, twelve years old when I was five,
my caretaker-playmate—your mother was dead,
Moll, your grandmother, stirring pots in our kitchen,
my mother dying.
                You say, as if in mourning,
that I am *family.* No explanation, just the word.
Family.   Familiar.   Famished.

New minted as lightning, apprehension tints
all remembrance with stormlight:
my grandmother's whispers, fifty years gone,
overheard once and meaningless then: *Moll's cabin*
she said, naming *terrible* and *shame,* naming
my grandfather's nephew *not gone*
till after sun-up. Those syllables
rolling away, lodged blue in the morning-
glory vine around the well, reddening
on the tomato plants, a dark weave
in the cock's crow and the lovely trill
of the peach orchard's mockingbird—
all strung now on frailest memory.

We are known only
in such mizzling light.

Now you sit down, smooth your dress.
We talk of your grandchildren,
my parents, your retirement
from the school cafeteria—
                everything but this.

Asides

September 11, 2001

On a sun-drenched street, one man looked up in time
to see hundreds of pigeons startle skyward just
before unbearable impact. Their reflection
shaped a flag of shadow on glass buildings
split-seconds before the image flew into shards,
a confetti of knives, and the birds
gone into a suddenly darkening sky.

It's said a woman in a Brooklyn kitchen turned
to see clouds in her window-glass, a backyard
filling with white paper, drifts of it shining
in sunlight but edged with the ink-black
of old-fashioned death letters. Beneath a sky
grown smokey with erasure, she turned toward
the new weather, alien snow bearing
the incomprehensible signatures of fire.

A man looked out an office window toward
other offices like his on another street,
felt close thunder first, and then—
for one tick of the clock—heard a huge
music he took to be beautiful, took to be
an inexplicable waterfall, gravity and silver
rivers at their play. Until he shivered
into seeing falling glass, the new Deluge.

All over Europe, and in Vietnam, in Russia,
China, Greece, Cambodia, Rwanda, Tibet—
were there answering shadows, a dimming
of light?
          Imperceptible ash, might the dead

of a century's wars have risen
like motes for a moment?
                              In the Hiroshima Museum
a sunshaft continued to bend, flowering again
and again within a vase of melted glass.
In countries made of blood-feud and sand,
didn't women turn from murmured prayers
toward the sky's answer, blank blue
point-blank burning glass?

And here, as in the slant light of every September,
caterpillars moved slowly along the turning leaves;
the cricket opened and shut his rusted door
into autumn; one particular firefly went out,
last low star of the season, indifferent
as a nova to what men have made.
                              Our marvelous
looking-glass holds, in its network of steel
and invisible signal, history and myth
and money laid across the world.
That great snare shines in its cables
like the orb-weaver's art, trembles fragile
as any web on night grass
                              in a field of starlight.

Ars Poetica *on an Island in the Cyclades*

Silence is part of what I want, but only
part. Too easy an exit, silence
collapses inward, can be nothing but posing,
another blind door heavy as irony.

      When words come
they should wear belief sheer
as a pair of wings, serious as the silver
on the underside of olive leaves
in April wind.
      Even the thyme
on the mountain utters a fragrance
meant to be known, and the goat
cries out his fear of becoming
a stone—all things are longing,
like lost children, for a path
as if through the rubble of war
(a path that is only the breath
and the music of breath),
a way back to themselves enlivened,
aghast, unrepentant, spoken anew.

Even that which crouches lifeless:
mineral or granite or empty seashell
desires to enter memory, given voice
even if only for the length of a syllable.

      My wish is to finish
with poems pale as their paper, to begin
with the letter *A,* to leave
nothing out.

That wish is formless, is only
a hope borne swaying on a boat
to one of the circle of islands flowering
on blue shawls of Aegean sky.
I bring with me a history
to be shredded like a poppy in the winds
of an older place. May I be so perfectly
torn as to come back with an alphabet
of shadows spelling

                where falls the sun.

The Poet Is Accused of Contradiction

You're right. Inside my skin
two women thrive. The days I live
are twice over, and the poems
double on their circle.

We fight. We dislike the color
of each other's eyes.
                    One pair of hands
is buried; one prays lightwise.

Neither can remember clearly
the red-dirt town we grew in,
its workings tiny as a toy village
its miniscule nightmares lurching
suddenly large as worlds—
though it is all we'll ever know.
                    We alternate belief
and laughter. See, she goes on
building, building what falls the way
shadows fall, story after tenebrous story.

One day, over a glass of dark wine,
we will admit each other and the red town
emptying, pooling between us like mud
in a graveyard, thumbprints
crusting its edges.

Letter to a Gifted Student

to Tim McBride

Know this first: the gift is worthless
you've been unwrapping all these years,
unlayering a Christmas paper gorgeous-patterned.
Or shroud-plain as clouds. Or soft dark
as velvet marked with wine or blood.

Each time, you'll keep the faith, *something
will turn up*—something material and sharp
as money: a knife, a pair of marble eyes,
a tree, a roofed pagoda, a bone, a flute.
Nothing ever does.

            Nothing does its dance
with you again: no paycheck, no crown
of laurel, no dragon slain, no downed
champagne. Just this unshading over and over,
the heart opened like a pomegranate, the compass

undone, landscape sunlit into ruin.
                    And the human
skin that holds it all so legible and fine?
Serpents are written there; or are they flowers?
Runes? Backlit tattoos, the long story
on the terrible lampshade?

No one will know you've opened this,
unlidded the box of music, susurrus
of leaves—an undoing you'll not cease
to do until words are all over
everything like birdsong or snow, a quilt
of locusts and asphalt and moonlight

all over and crumbling.
And you still here,
                    unwrapping the disappearing
small rain, the one
                    serviceable tear.

Anomaly

Child, go careful down
these lazy walks
where the sun wears easy birds
for your delighted seeing.
Sharp song wears a beak.

Child, go watchful through
the cornered sleep
where night is warm, and light's
a texture of your roof.
Stars can hide and darkness
grow a tooth.

In all your winging days,
in the close curve of dream,
hearts are hunting.
You will hear your own
go with them when they come
starved and well meaning.

Uncaged love is running
free here. Child, go cunning.

SOME LIGHT

Short Takes

KNEE

Neither too high nor too low,
a place on the way, unkissed
small island nobody remembers to visit.

DESERT BEYOND GIZA

I sent myself this letter the color
of lions. It moves by bitter light
in a language that stings the eyes.
Isn't this what I came for,
what I always wanted?

TO AN OLD LOVE

You were in my life like rain.
Now I have a house and an indoor garden.
The silence takes up most of my time.
It is like a child without a tongue,
fretful, knowing everything.

NEW

The red lizard moves on his stone
like a clock hand. The shadows
deepen and the world completes
a lidless change.

Two Poems with One Epigraph

Poets can finesse the invitation to infinite irony, which
Paul De Man shows haunts the dramatic lyric.
—Charles Altieri

1

A critic also can finesse
an invitation, and digress.
So the early Paul de Man,
before he turned his tail and ran,
lent his printed sympathies
to the darker Nazi theories
then found a different territory
(specifically, the Literary)
where he lived well until he died,
otherwise quite occupied.

2

No lyric drama can resist
the ubiquitous deconstructionist.
But lyric's short, and irony
is longer far than current theory.

What else could the man who wrote
for Nazis do but cut the throat
of meaning everywhere, and render
language an illegal tender?

If words are nothing but a text
talking to another text,
he needn't worry that he vexed

God and man with words. The fit
of this shoe to the careful foot
of the man who praised the boot
is perfect. Iron. Infinite.

Names

My real name is Elizabeth, so right for a poet:
sensitive, half of a great love,
consumptive, even diaphanous—
like a peignoir. Or
beautifully strict: say, Miss Bishop
on the way to visit Miss Moore.

How could my mother (understandably
fearing *Lizzie*) have so shortened
my possibilities? At fifteen,
I knew I was an Elizabeth,
but nobody listened.
                How awful
to be *Betty*, all aprons and frosting mix,
thirties cartoons, fifties pinups,
boop-boop-be-doops and va-vooms.
It's a name for a waitress, a bowler, a clerk
in a store, a housewife, an apple dessert.

It is never, ever, the name of a poet.
        And yet . . . and yet,
doesn't poetry have to be every bit as tough
as the woman pouring diner coffee?
as practical as the mother of several
who tends bar, does laundry, and cooks?
It has to sing a little, toe the line
like a dancer, and good looks won't hurt it.
It has to rise and shine and be able
to clear a table and make change
in a New York minute.

And poetry, compared to prose,
is darker, richer, sweeter—
a chocolate-frosting birthday-cake rose.

And though we all wanted to be Plath or Sexton
(at least for part of the way), dying
isn't really a prerequisite,
nor is the peignoir, the grand obsession
with one or more lovers.
And you don't really have to be a professor.
Wouldn't I rather roll a strike at a bowling alley
than bowl them over in the faculty lounge with theory?

So maybe the poet I am
                              is not an Elizabeth
despite the name on my birth certificate.
Perhaps I was nicked into consciousness
and my true calling.
                              After all,
what could be odder than a woman poet from Texas?
Give her a trash name too and there's just no telling
what she might do, aiming for Parnassus
and the solar plexus.

Three Dated Love Poems Found in a Drawer

1967

There is never more than one place to be,
it arrives each time with a different map,
sun on the moss, my life running
over my hands like water, pure
animal that won't be caught.

1973

I have been still, lying straight
as a track some other motion takes.
I seem to have disappeared into the color
of metal. Don't be fooled. Like the rain-star
on the rose I come back, my love,
a bone in the throat. If you break
my mirror where it wrinkles
(that ripple in the dreaming lake)
I'll sing the closing of water.
If you love me you have to remember
what I remember. Your luck
has nothing to do with this.

1984

If I am permitted to stop singing,
I will speak simple stories: a farmer
watches the crows pass up his harvest,
their black wings merciful, lovely
as oil on water. That good-bye is the language
I want, not this machinery, this dancing

in red shoes. If I am permitted to stop,
I will touch this scalded world
with words plain as rainfall,
apples, wool, bread, knives.

Coda 2003

Never trust the early work. These poems
duck the issues, run every which way
away with themselves, regarding their own images
with such fascination they're apt to fall in
and likely to drown in reflection.
Let's take them back to their beginnings,
check into a motel somewhere, tell them
to take off their clothes.

Gladys in Springtime

Always in a pale dress or one just touched
with pastel flowers, she never
quite speaks. She's the Amen
in the flesh of two chins, and atremble,
body square as a hen coop,
the flutter within.

She has no opinions. She has
an orange cat and a china closet,
a vegetable garden, pans of brown biscuits,
Christ crucified and a plumb husband.
All her flowerbeds bloom on time.
She has tunneled through, a diligent mole.
Tied up in a scarf, she goes—

and it is all behind her, the world,
whatever might have been,
that little breathy tune
heard once, returning dim, absurd
in the curves of her red tulips,
in the rolled summer-to-come
of the nasturtium.

House Cats

for Caroline and David

Think how their ancestors came to flicker
at temple fires, to stare and disappear
like fugitive smoke. Now, they are silks
winding among the backyard shrubbery,
around our ankles, running their bright quick
paths through the weave of everyday.

What have we done to deserve them?—
wild as they are, connected as they are
to the riddle of sparrow snatched out of air,
and the riddle of darkness, the riddle
of invisibility.
                    Those who love them
have reason. Those who fear them
have reason.

We know you, they say, charming us
with a look the color of Egypt.
And they are two-natured: sun and moon,
wind and fire, diamond and shadow.
They may touch with velvet or with needles
stitching us in place. They still us
with the thrumming reverie of their throats
just before they leap outward, comets
in the backyard's firmament.

Imagine the crossings, the pilgrimage
of bridges these creatures daily undertake
between the worlds.
                    Between prehistory
and the pillow: between our version

of ourselves and the one they know,
the one we dare not quite remember.
Between death
                    and its translation into love
they launch themselves, reminding us how sharp
is the language of praise.

Once my daughter asked if it was wrong to pray
for her dying Tabby. *Children are suffering
in every country.* It isn't wrong;
it's wise not to weigh such losses—
sorrow is sorrow, the going away
of any part of things.

And the cat is kin to everything, even
the feathered risings, bright blood lifted
skyward; and sings of molten indolence,
and of fog that hides a movement. The least
leaf aloft in a breeze is to be rushed
and perused. Likewise the whispered
secrets of the deepest kingdoms
of mole and chipmunk and gopher.

Think of the way a cat becomes
another thing: the inside
of a small dark place, a momentary ribbon
of wind, a blade of light. All metaphor,
that body converts into liquid,
into mist, into wit, into shine!

Will die in its time without
once crying out, eyes
jeweled with reflections:
temple fires, old blessings.

"It's déjà vu all over again"

—Yogi Berra

Having exhausted soul, spirit, and "made in the image
of God," what's left for us but to become
material sans mage.

                   Life and cosmos are one,
asserts the new cosmologist, and we of course
are life's only definition, parsed
by simply being what we are.

        "If we're alone in the universe,
        whether we survive or not
        determines whether there's a point
        to the rest of cosmic history."
        — *New York Times Book Review*

The wise cosmologist has made his book to show
why colonies of us in space are mandatory,
a project to rest in the hands of good Bill Gates
and similar rich adventurers who can pay.
Oh gates of paradise! Or purgatory.

So we're the point of all of it. Didn't we always know it?
That no tree can fall without us?
Still, there's the old rat's tooth of doubt.
We fear if all things human one day fail to wake,
cosmos might *not* vanish. Nor future lose its sharpest point.
As we've needed others, we need the scientist to make
believe we do exist for Heaven's sake.

Housekeeping

We bought a roofed box for birds.
They never came. We nailed it higher
in the oak, and got for tenants
one dark, unspecified snake,
a bat the color of cinnamon,
and finally, a flying squirrel
with regular habits.
No wings unless you count the squirrel's
gliding skin or the bat's leather.
The snake, of course, was earlier.

In another house I was learning never
to quarrel with means of ascension.
Let rise whatever will, in whatever
way is possible.
                Or several.

Poem to a Friend Explaining Why I Did Not Attend the Convention of Professional Poets

The brushpile on our hill trembles
with a fever of cardinals.
A thin sun still hones an edge
on the mornings when sky is the color
of stone dust. In these last days
of winter, it is always possible
some small animals will leave their harbors
out of season, setting off across fields
that are dark with cold, that sing
not easily, having for bells
only the owls half given to silence.
Those who begin here, leaving dim footprints,
know a path only the narrowest moon
can recite: the one moment graced with the given,
the one line stammering with light.

PLACES

Source

Morning falls starless, pale, a rain
of January's thin enlightenment among
our trees whitelined with snow.

Nothing rosy-fingered, this dawn is more
a solemn afterword, the story over.
Yet is it not also a fever,
this stone *no*?

Cold's palette frays the cloudbank's ash
with peach, with low violet like a hum,
and that blush-pink some glass will turn
left long enough deep underground.

But really it's the pair of cobalt shears
the bluejay wields that cuts flat gray;
the cardinal's sudden flame that sets
a backyard's dark asunder, making visible
the squirrel's dimpled run in snow
and the dog's mazed tracings. Here,
God's a minimalist:

lines fierce and simple, colors singular,
a sharpening to light that comes of no
slow cauldron spilling cloud-high,
but in small quick bursts, and low—
in the white-throated sparrow's drop of yellow,
the russet lifting from the towhee's side;
even grackle's iridescence and the woodpecker's
red penny are spent against dark air that is
now lit, now lilting, day welling up,
overspilling from its earthen bed
here, among the dying.

Anniversary

for Don

In every summer I remember there were bees
                hiving the columns of the porch. A cliché
                even then, the house sat like a tiered cake
                fading on its hill, an antique joke.

Winter-long in high-ceilinged rooms, I'd freeze
                and every June the wet, sweet heat began
                wrapping everything so close you'd seem to lose
                all ability to move. Then everybody had to
                wear summer like a second, leaden skin.

The house was garrisoned with cedars, ancients
                whose branches crashed in the least wind.
                Don't you walk under the cedar trees, I'd hear again,
                watching bright blue flags of sky aglitter
                between the heavy limbs, my face straight up
                and risking, Grandmother shouting from the kitchen.

You and I were married in that house one June,
                wedding party afraid of bee stings, terrified
                our guests would faint in the seethe of kin.
                But the flowers did not quite die of fever,
                and the stairs held as we walked down together
                forever. The way people tried too hard to walk back then.
                And nothing fell on us as we drove afterward
                under old trees into the dark all ceremonies hide.

Now is our summer anniversary.
        We took the risks, or didn't, as they came.
        I took some journeys. You did. The child is grown.
        Grandchildren center our new orrery.
        We wrote one name.

I think a smoke-wisp, some small flag
        of us stays by that house,
        something bright and clear as we were,
        marrying in the unintended scent of sweat and honey.
        Imagine us: ghost banners, held breaths
        where the cedar trees are gone, the house undone.

Remember how, on a long hike years ago,
        we discovered a fleet of daffodils
        sailing still in a place the woods had taken?
        They had come back (how many springs?)
        to signal where a house had vanished,
        a well caved in. Those yellow echoes circled
        what once was, as if nothing can quite vanquish
        the print of human having-been.

We'll toast that night the two of us began
        to stay. We'll start the way we ran,
        trusting the sky-blue behind a night
        in the arms of dangerous histories
        old winds blow through;
                    though our daffodils
        are yet invisible, and the bees with their honey
        are elsewhere.

Rare

Leavenworthia texana . . . found only in the southeast
corner of San Augustine County, Texas.
—*Nature Conservancy* notes

Losing ground, this obscure East Texas county's
gone into its past like a wintering plant,
its one town shrinking inward, root-cut.

Beyond the empty streets, one farm—enisled—
rests on strange erosions, outcrops of the Eocene,
greensand clay under calcareous sediment

that holds more fossils from the ancient seas
than any place on this Deep Southern coast.
What died here was immense, was measureless.

What dies here now is negligible to compare:
songs, a forest, a lilt of speech, and violence
in the ways to farm and worship, to kill, to cure

the meat. Churches and small stores once bloomed
with people and raw goods on a roiling sea
of the dark history that lived on. Now

the depths are gone. The South's crooked anomalies,
like beached creations of another world, have built
in dying a land no one can till.

Now, on my great-grandfather's farm, on fossilized
remains of the longest prologue, this
unspectacular blossom: Texas golden gladecress.

Leavenworthia texana flowers in February,
a tiny yellow burgeoning for the narrow
days between winter and spring. Sharply bright,

endangered, useless, almost too low to see,
it's visible only on close inspection
of the common ground; is found in this one archival

soil, nowhere else on earth. Like poetry,
it thrives in contradiction,
one of the small, acute survivals.

World Enough

As if he had a birthday every week
(now that he forgets how many winters
have knotted in his bones), his sons
and daughters bring their saccharin talk

and grandchildren exhibited as gifts
whose use he cannot guess.
Soft words and hands, soft candy, fruit—
he answers them with silence they can't lift.

His body, waked from long health's sleep,
has grown wild and important, has become deep
as the forest his childhood roamed, familiar keep,
now with a new moon and stranger rocks and beasts.

The window in his room's a landscape drilled
into the wall he doesn't see. He sees dark red
behind his eyelids, sees briars and toothless ruins,
the crouch of hungry light behind a hill

that might be dream or prophecy or time.
He wanders a maze of paths, a lifeline of scars.
An island riding a sheeted sea, he bears
some secret talisman through plunge and climb.

He knows the only ground there is, is flesh.
His children, smoke from old campfires, vanish,
thinning past the distances where one
finger of sunlight brightens into voice—

a woman's, the only not-himself he gropes to know.
Who is she? She sets him and the dank bed shaking.
Mother? Wife? A touchless, shining girl a life ago?
He rubs his handful of dust; he starts the making.

First Trip

1971

Staying with Americans, I am almost
not here at all.
              It's the first time.
Our plane descended in morning light,
the Andes coming true, great walls
we sank between.

One vermouth in Quito's air
spun the whole afternoon to gauze,
blurring the Galapagos turtles grazing
on the lawn of the exclusive club,
dulling the market's fruits,
the rainbows of tiny potatoes,
the children, one with a running eye.
Chula buses ajostle with people
and goats, birds and flowers, rocked
and plummeted along steep streets.

What did I see?
It was the first time: *Oh, let
this be that other world itself,*
I might have prayed that evening,
watching from my second-floor window
in the home of friends. Behind a stumbling
fence, a *zapatería*—the shoe repairman working,
his wife at a tub of clothes, seven
children chasing geese among the vegetables.

Which game did not stop, their play or my trying
to see? *Oh that,* my friend said, *that*

will be torn down, perhaps by spring.
I remember blue and red shirts on the line,
the white geese trying to fly. I brought home
only the *zapatería* and the sudden
thin air of the mountains.

Aegean Notes

Mountain pasture
                rough wall of rock and schist
one horse the color of dawn
                      the light washes over:
invisible horse.

Winding low walls mortarless have held
for centuries, meditations perhaps
on the weight of millennia. When
a truck knocked this one down, one man
brought only his craftsman's hands
to the flexible remaking. Like memory:
same stones,
               different pattern.

Island wind
               unpredictable lover,
wine-breath and a skittish heart.
                       May sun
has blown the roses full
                too soon
a churchyard riot of tumbling blooms
timeless as Renaissance paintings
in the golden
               sway of this place.

The *Phlaros* has three spouts for pouring
olive-wood smoke, libations
against the gods of winter. This clay
chimney decants, in a disappearing
script, archaic fire.

A century has left no more mark
than the claws of wild thyme
gnawing the pathless mountain.

Rebetika. This music has roads instead of scales.

The whole island is a church:
altar after white altar masquerades
as house or shed or dovecote set
among the terraced fields, the whole
blue dome of heaven overseeing,
gathering even the face of the sea
to reflection.
Two-throated bells open and close
the day as a holy book.
Outside the monastery, five bells
green with time hang in a tree.
A nun made entirely of shadow
materializes behind a gate of iron lace
to pull five ropes, to pull down the light:
now every bell in the village tolls
rich with the streaming sacrament

of the sun, round and recall
of the bloody past that now
can settle briefly into praise.

      ✶

Late at night the donkeys' voices voyage
a grievous dark, little boats of despair
adrift toward anchors of patient silence.

      ✶

Medicine pouch
             this journal is
music box
            egg basket
wineskin for carrying this place,
the whole scrap and scree and scrim
I've come to know
           (though words
can carry nothing, we're told)
the way we knew our faces before
there were any mirrors.

                    Sifnos, Greece

To Mollie Siju Ruinsky, Granddaughter in the Air

adopted in China, December 2003

In your fifteenth month on earth,
flying asleep into frangible darkness
and a stranger dawn, you're the child
in a story flying enchanted, enchanting
the family taking hold of your future.

Father and mother newfashioned
and the sister who came this way before
are asleep on thin air; all four
dream the radiance you must lose—
one whole day vanished!

                      That lost light
will stay as with ghosts in the place
where the Han River and the Yangtze converse.
Imagine in the absent sun of Wuhan, your new family
and all your blood kin may meet, passing through
one another in mythtime, dream time.
Your sister turns in her sleep. She is five;
she remembers her own leap, light spilled
on the airborne threshold.

You can bring with you only the name *Siju*
and the ragged stuffed mouse you hold on to.
Homemade, oddly outsized in its dress
of incongruous gingham, this talisman
is deepest companion. It has protected
your sleep with its touch, your play
with its knowing whiskers, its chewed
ears, and the tail that's gone missing.

We praise the mouse torn for love.
It will dampen with tears in the night
after night you will wake
into fearful American darkness, almost
remembering something, a shining.
Almost.
        For now you are sleeping aloft
in your claim on us, our future
like the dawn rising through you.
Siju, you are nearly,
                    nearly here.

Kind of Blue

A dusk-blue heron stalks the steady melody
of our backyard pond, wings like a riff of twilight.
He settles to stand, an uneasy column of smoke,
in the sun's eddy.

He isn't quite the tune, which is suburban,
smallish, whittled down by highway drone.
He's part of it, though, blue being
a heaviness becoming longing.
He answers our shallows with transfiguring
attention, a bent listening that is itself
a singing.
                    Why not? blue's blue.

Every midnight scatters its spotlights
on such intricate shapings elsewhere: loss
counted on reed and horn and bass-string,
a flute's long straw sipping shadow,
sax cultivating double-cross.

The dictionary publishes *blue* this way:
Said of the color of vapor, of smoke
and distant hills, of thin milk and steel;
said of the pale flame without red
which is seen as an omen for ghosts.

The blues always did get around.

If metaphor
is motive for change, then this bird marooned
among cars and dogs and clumsy tract houses

is part mist and shade and cloud, is mountain
distance, milky dawn, part steel-domed
sleepless night, and is a ghost-flame
vigilant against the rows of ranch-house roofs
that line the last deep spill of sunset
on a wingspan of low blue sky.

Solo

we won't forget.

Chimneys: A History of Deep East Texas

Built 1832

Dobber chimney, they called this kind
made of mayhaw mud and Spanish moss.
From a distance it must have seemed
something placed by giant wasps
with wings of smoke: their nest
with a human house nailed up beside.

To build it, men stomped barefoot in wet clay
and moss-thatch, working, working earth,
and molding by hand the heavy *cats*
tossed up to other men high-balanced
on a simple framework of sticks.

Humblest, most vital house part—like the sex
of a creature it was needed, was the passionate
center of lives in which fire made the meat
and all else possible, even the bear
clawing under the door
                    for succor or murder.

Built 1844

Hacked and hauled to this stoneless place,
matched mortarless and held perfect
by nothing but form and gravity,
its stones have stayed.
                    And though a new fire might kill
who tried it, the old are black and righteous
in that stone throat.

In the still shut air of a dogtrot life,
wild joy, wild grief, and moveless loneliness
were breathed up, breathed out into gray
or star-filled sky, into storm or golden
summer heat—with the smell of cooked meat.
Animals that were spitted here, and the long-gone
man and woman (generation on generation)
who fretted again and again against
this life, or loved or raged in it,
are a faint fat in the soot's heart.

Built 1900

Here five brick chimneys held the breath
of comfort. Five fireplaces bore carved mantels
for clocks and candlesticks and Christmas greens.
Their paler smoke was a courteous scrim
of plenty. It reached higher—like the answered
prayers of the wealthy—though the fires
of these blessed were required, also, to die.

Choice

Saved fragment of my father's
only chapel, fragrant stillness among high
trees pinned to September's perfect sky—
light falls here more softly than summer's.

Towers of ambition, a few big pines have toppled
like temple columns, long mysteries forgotten.
One massive oak, pulled altogether out
by some relentless wind, has taken with it
companion saplings, dogwoods growing sidelong
from great knots of ripped-up earth and roots,
living on to spring again their delicate,
precipitate promises.

No heavenward soaring, just this

                             grounded life,
slantwise, burgeoning and brief.

Notes

1. "Fallen" (page 31): The disintegration of the space shuttle *Columbia* was reported primarily from larger towns where more of the ship's debris fell (e.g., Nacogdoches, where twisted metal parts landed in the streets). In adjacent San Augustine County, however, remains of the astronauts themselves fell in remote woods, along with pieces of the spacecraft. The macabre details were understandably not covered in the national news, but the information in the poem is accurate and comes from private local sources and corroborating photographs.

Bourne means both boundary and destination.

2. "Asides" (page 36): The first three stanzas contain material from interviews with New Yorkers on National Public Radio after the disaster.

3. "Kind of Blue" (page 77) is the title of a famous jazz album recorded by trumpeter Miles Davis in 1959.

4. "Chimneys: A History of Deep East Texas" (page 79): A *cat-and-clay* was originally a large roll of straw and clay worked together and shaped. The term was shortened colloquially (as here) to *cat*.

Dogtrot refers to the hall, roofed but open at both ends, between the two rooms of early southern cabins. Its name tells one of its uses. The other was excellent ventilation in a hot climate.